MANHATTAN

A PICTORIAL SOUVENIR

CAROL M. HIGHSMITH AND TED LANDPHAIR

MANHATTAN
A PICTORIAL SOUVENIR

CRESCENT BOOKS

NEW YORK

THE AUTHORS GRATEFULLY ACKNOWLEDGE
THE SERVICES, ACCOMMODATIONS, AND SUPPORT PROVIDED BY
HILTON HOTELS CORPORATION
AND
THE NEW YORK HILTON
IN CONNECTION WITH THE COMPLETION OF THIS BOOK.

THE AUTHORS ALSO WISH TO THANK THE MARK HOTEL AND THE
NEW YORK CONVENTION AND VISITORS BUREAU FOR THEIR GENEROUS
ASSISTANCE AND HOSPITALITY DURING THEIR VISITS TO MANHATTAN.

———

PAGES 2–3: *The skyline of the West Side of Midtown Manhattan forms a stately backdrop to drab factory buildings and oil tanks for those who drive to the city from the south via the New Jersey side of the Hudson River. Train travelers, however, appear in the midst of "Gotham," with all of its soaring towers, as if by magic after emerging from Penn Station.*

This 1998 edition is published by Crescent Books, a division of Random House Value Publishing, Inc., 201 East 50th Street, New York, N.Y. 10022.

Crescent Books and colophon are registered trademarks of Random House Value Publishing, Inc.

Random House
New York • Toronto • London • Sydney • Auckland
http://www.randomhouse.com/

Printed and bound in China

Library of Congress Cataloging-in-Publication Data
Highsmith, Carol M., 1946–
Manhattan / Carol M. Highsmith and Ted Landphair.
p. cm. — (Pictorial souvenir)
ISBN 0-517-18762-0
1. Manhattan (New York, N.Y.)—Tours. 2. Manhattan (New York, N.Y.)—Pictorial works. 3. New York (N.Y.)—Tours. 4. New York (N.Y.)—Pictorial works. I. Landphair, Ted, 1942– . II. Series: Highsmith, Carol M., 1946– Pictorial souvenir.
F128.18.H52 1998
917.47´10443´0222—dc21 97-18034
CIP

8 7 6 5 4 3 2

———

Project Editor: Donna Lee Lurker
Production Supervisor: Richard Willett
Designed by Robert L. Wiser, Archetype Press, Inc., Washington, D.C.

FOREWORD

New York City is the planet's second-largest city, behind London. The heart of New York is the borough of Manhattan. To this day, the world assumes that this island—a half mile long and two and a half miles wide at its widest point—*is* New York City. Peter Minuit, the Dutch West India Company's director, bought the island from Native Americans for sixty guilders' worth of goods (about one thousand dollars at today's value) in 1626. The English took over the city in 1644, but it remained a polyglot, for-profit venture. Commerce, not idealism, drove the settlers, who even in the earliest days spoke more than a dozen different languages. With trade came banks, insurance companies, investment houses, wharves, and factories.

When F. Scott Fitzgerald first beheld the city in 1919, he remarked that it "had all the iridescence of the beginning of the world." It was a Manhattan skyline adorned with towering skyscrapers, a metropolis of unsurpassed modern architectural grandeur. The island's most famous buildings include the astounding seventy-seven-story Art Deco Chrysler Building built in 1930, and the 102-story Empire State Building, built a year later, which has become the architectural metaphor for the mightiest city on earth.

The writer Robert Alden called Manhattan "the cockpit of...commercial interchange." Two powerful stock exchanges, Wall Street brokerage houses, international banks and insurance companies, prestigious law firms, and the headquarters of some of the world's largest retailers and other corporations are located on the island. It is also the communications capital of the world, headquarters of television networks, the home office of two of the world's great newspapers—the *New York Times* and the *Wall Street Journal*—as well as the home of the world's largest publishers of books and magazines.

Manhattan also has one of the world's oldest subways which opened in 1904 and is now a system of twenty-five lines, carrying more than 3.6 million passengers daily. Another wonder that Manhattanites take pride—and pleasure—in is Central Park, an 843-acre playland of lawns, gardens, ponds, paths, castles, skating rinks, small amusement parks, and even a zoo.

Manhattan is also the entertainment and cultural center of the world. In addition to the fabled theaters of Broadway, there is the giant Metropolitan Museum of Art, the largest such institution in the Western Hemisphere, and the cornerstone of "Museum Mile" that includes the Frick Collection, the Guggenheim modern-art museum, and the Whitney Museum of American Art. Across town is the American Museum of Natural History, the Museum of American Folk Art, and Lincoln Center that houses the Metropolitan and New York City opera companies, the New York Philharmonic, the New York City Ballet and the American Ballet Theatre, and the Julliard School of Music.

Manhattan is also the haven of distinct neighborhoods including the galleries and cozy lofts of SoHo and TriBeCa, the bohemian enclaves of Greenwich Village and the East Village, and the ethnic color of Harlem, Chinatown, and Little Italy.

There's never a lack of something to do, someplace to go, someone to see on this island of 1.5 million residents, a million more workers, and half a million weekly visitors. Manhattan, a world capital of not only finance, culture, diplomacy, and communications, but of sheer excitement as well.

OVERLEAF: The outlined silhouette at the center is South Street Seaport. Beneath the city's six thousand miles of streets run sixty-two thousand miles of electrical wires and conduits.

The South Street Seaport Museum (left and above) was a creation of the Rouse Company in cooperation with the city's Public Development Corporation. Whole blocks off Fulton Street were made into a "festival marketplace" shopping and dining complex that retains vestiges of the waterfront wharves and fish market.

Trinity Church (right) at Broadway and Wall Street, designed by Richard Upjohn, rose in 1846. Its three massive bronze doors were created by Richard Morris Hunt. They recall Ghiberti's doors on the Baptistry in Florence. The AIA Guide to New York *called the structure an "anthracite jewel," so dark was its color, but a 1991 restoration of the sandstone revealed the church's color is pink. New Yorkers Alexander Hamilton, the nation's first treasury secretary, and Robert Fulton, inventor of the steamboat, are among the notables buried in the Trinity Church graveyard (opposite) in the city's Wall Street section. The spire of the church itself was the tallest structure in town, visible for miles on Manhattan and from Brooklyn and Queens, until the first skyscraper was built in 1887.*

Arturo DiModica's three-and-a-half-ton bronze Charging Bull (above), sculpted in response to the stock market slump of 1987, has become a symbol of New York's Wall Street. The New York Stock Exchange floor (opposite) is a nonstop, and now high-tech, beehive of activity. About two hundred million shares of stock are traded each day here, now more often by computer than by shouts from frenzied brokers. OVERLEAF: From the East River, the twin 110-story towers of the World Trade Center— just two of five office buildings in the complex—hover over the rest of Lower Manhattan. The elevator in Two World Trade Center takes just fifty-eight seconds to reach the 107th-floor observation deck. Another in One World Trade Center is just as speedy to the Windows on the World restaurant.

Cass Gilbert's older, more ornate Ninety West Street Building stands in marked contrast to the World Trade Center towers (above). The smaller limestone-and-terracotta office building was erected in 1907. OPPOSITE: More than twenty workers died building the Brooklyn Bridge, the world's first steel suspension bridge—including its German-born designer, engineer John Roebling. Many laborers suffered attacks of the bends working in the underwater caissons that became footings for the bridge's towers. Each weekday morning and afternoon, there's a rush-hour scramble on the bridge, not only involving automobiles but also among the thousands of pedestrians and bicyclists heading to work and home across its span. Built from 1867 to 1883, the bridge helped spur the development of "Greater New York" that swallowed Brooklyn and three other new "boroughs" into the expanded New York City.

Galleries, clothing and curio shops, grocery stores, and restaurants abound in Chinatown (right), which has expanded from three to more than forty square blocks. Its more than 150,000 residents make New York's Chinatown not only larger than San Francisco's, but also the largest Chinese community outside of Asia. Tortuously narrow and crooked streets are especially crowded around Chinese New Year in mid-winter. There's a Chinatown History Museum at the corner of Bayard and Mulberry streets whose collections highlight Asian Americans' labor history. But Chinese restaurants are by no means confined to Chinatown. China Fun (above) on Columbus Avenue, for one, introduced several "fusion" dishes combined from different cultures, including seafood papillote and various kinds of barbecued meats.

The size of Little Italy (above) has shrunk as Chinatown expands. Savory holdouts, including restaurants, cheese shops, and delicatessens, can be found along Mulberry Street. Little Italy's first residents—immigrant laborers and their families from the southern Italian peninsula—were crammed together in "dumbbell apartments" covering seventeen square blocks. These tenements were built so close together that sunlight could not even reach their courtyards. SoHo's Greene Street (opposite) is a warren of antique shops, studios, and loft apartments in converted tenement buildings. The district includes the largest surviving concentration of cast-iron-fronted architecture in the world. Saving many of these buildings from demolition in the path of a proposed Lower Manhattan Expressway was one of preservationists' greatest achievements. Fire escapes were too often an afterthought: so numerous were the conflagrations in warehouses filled with flammables that the neighborhood was called "Hell's Hundred Acres."

Washington Square (left) grew up on a former potter's field and parade ground. Stanford White executed its magnificent marble arch in 1895 to replace a wooden arch that had marked the centennial of George Washington's first inauguration downtown. Many former mansions on "The Row" across the street have been taken over by New York University. ABOVE: A homeless artist created the impromptu sculpture in front of the offices of the Village Voice, which publishes a comprehensive list of events in TriBeCa, SoHo, and Greenwich Village. OVERLEAF: In Greenwich Village, rents that were once cheap attracted writers like Walt Whitman and Edgar Allan Poe, and artists like Albert Bierstadt and John La Farge.

PREVIOUS PAGES: Seen from the Queens shore, the Midtown Manhattan skyline shows some breaks in the skyscrapers. The United Nations Secretariat is at the left, the Chrysler Building's lighted, stainless-steel tower splits the frame, and other U.N. buildings appear along the waterfront.

ABOVE: New York Governor Samuel Tilden so feared his opponents in the Tweed Ring that he had rolling steel doors built into his Gramercy Park home. The building, with its lovely stonework detail, now houses the National Arts Club.

RIGHT: Chicago architect Daniel Burnham's 1902 Fuller Building overlooking Madison Square—later renamed the Flatiron Building because of its wedge shape—is only six feet wide at its apex. OPPOSITE: The National Park Service operates Theodore Roosevelt's birthplace on East Twentieth Street. The original house was destroyed but later faithfully reconstructed by Theodate Pope Riddle as a memorial to the energetic president.

Haunted houses are commonplace across America, but not haunted restaurants. Looking at the condition of the "doormen," one has to wonder about the Jekyll and Hyde Club "for Eccentric Explorers and Mad Scientists" (above) on Seventh Avenue. RIGHT: Carnegie Hall was built in 1891, when Pyotr Ilich Tchaikovsky conducted the New York Philharmonic's opening concert. The hall's acoustics are legendary, though some purists argue that they will never match the pristine sound prior to extensive renovation for its centennial. A museum was added, chronicling the auditorium's illustrious performances, not only by classical-music geniuses but also by popular musicians like Count Basie and Benny Goodman.

When the white
marble and stone
Saint Patrick's
Cathedral (opposite)
was built in the late
1870s and named for
the patron saint of
Ireland, parishioners
scoffed at the location,
far up Fifth Avenue at
Fiftieth Street, out in
the "country." Many
wanted to put a grave-
yard on the site
instead, but Arch-
bishop John Hughes
prevailed and bought
land from the city
for $83. Architect
James Renwick Jr.'s
French Gothic
creation would soon
be regarded as New
York's finest Gothic
structure. Its twin
spires rise 330 feet
across from Rockefeller
Center. RIGHT: The
1872 Moorish-style
Central Synagogue on
Lexington Avenue is
the oldest continually
used Jewish synagogue
in the city. It was
designed by Henry
Fernbach, the
nation's first promi-
nent Jewish architect.

Henry Hardenbergh, who had designed the Dakota apartment building and the Waldorf-Astoria Hotel, designed the French Renaissance–style Plaza Hotel (opposite). It included extensive apartments for the Rockefellers and other prominent New York families. Fifth Avenue (above) has become synonymous with wealth and high society. As high-end jewelry and department stores gradually moved up the avenue, they displaced—or moved into—some of the city's finest mansions. An aggressive merchants' association helped to sustain the elegance of Fifth Avenue by keeping out billboards, parking lots, and street vendors. No "els" clattered by, either; instead there were an independent Fifth Avenue Transportation Company's horse-drawn omnibuses, followed later by open-top double-deck buses. Though only four of the latter existed, they were fondly remembered when they disappeared, especially since the grand ride up the avenue cost no more than a subway ride.

Macy's (left), the
world's largest depart-
ment store, was
founded by a former
whaler. It covers a full
city block down West
Thirty-fourth Street
from the Empire State
Building. Fashion
trends for much of the
nation are set in the
city's Garment
District, now called
the Fashion Center.
The series of produc-
tion warehouses,
showrooms, and
workshops has been
pinpointed by a street
statue of a garment
worker (above) on
Seventh Avenue.
New York's "rag trade"
employed East
European Jews, then
gradually Asians,
Hispanics, and other
immigrants, some-
times in deplorable
sweatshops, first on
the Lower East Side,
then in the Thirties
on the West Side.
Faced with increasing
international compe-
tition, responsible
industry leaders have
worked to expose and
correct such conditions
as well as clean up
and better patrol the
neighborhood.

Jules-Alexis Coutans's sculpture of Mercury, Hercules, and Minerva crowns the main entrance of the 1913 Grand Central Terminal (right), which blocks Park Avenue. The commuter station was meticulously restored in the early 1990s. The New York Life Insurance Company's building on Madison Avenue (above), designed in 1928 by Cass Gilbert, was built on the site of the first Madison Square Garden. Only after train lines were buried did Park Avenue (overleaf) attain its status as the city's boulevard of posh hotels, private palaces, and apartment buildings—perhaps the world's priciest strip of real estate. Several expensive office towers have been added to the avenue.

CENTRAL
MINAL

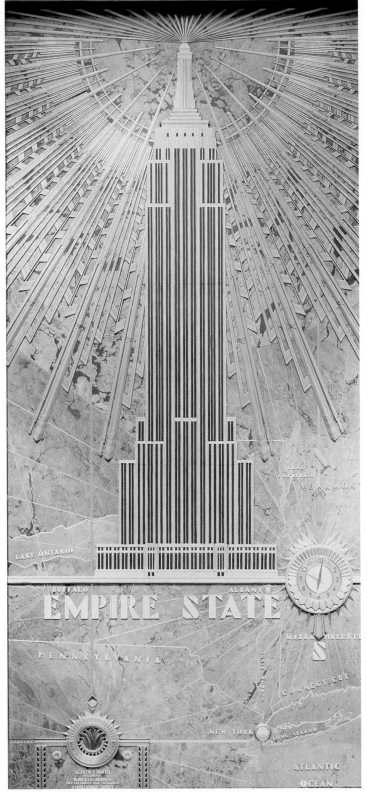

PREVIOUS PAGES: Television person-alities still keep late hours in and around the Ed Sullivan Theater on Broadway. In its lobby, the Empire State Building (right) salutes itself as the "Eighth Wonder of the World." The building (above) included a tower designed— but never used— to moor zeppelins. Its 102nd-floor obser-vatory became a hot tourist destination. William Van Alen's seventy-seven-story Art Deco Chrysler Building (opposite), clad in stainless steel, combined practical engineering and stunning decoration and it typified the race to be the world's tallest building: its shining spire was hidden in the fire shaft until the unveiling, then dra-matically raised to give it supremacy over a bank building down-town. But it was the world's tallest for only a few months, until the Empire State Building opened. The Chrysler Building's fluorescent lancet crown glimmers over the New York skyline at night.

Begun during the
Great Depression of
the 1930s, Rockefeller
Center became the
city's "second down-
town." It combines
nineteen entertain-
ment, shopping, and
office buildings, with
the towering General
Electric Building
(above) at its hub.
Underground passage-
ways connect the
center's restaurants,
network television
studios, doctors'
offices, boutiques,
banks, and publishers'
headquarters. The rink
at Rockefeller Center
(right) is a popular
cold-weather attrac-
tion. It gives way to
an outdoor restaurant
in warmer months
and is towered over
by a huge Christmas
tree each Yuletide.
Paul Manship created
the Prometheus
statue in 1934.

The United Nations complex (opposite) was designed by an international committee, led by American Wallace Harrison. It sits on land that once supported Turtle Bay farms, then squalid tenement houses. Today it is technically international territory—there is even an American Embassy on the property! The familiar glass-walled tower houses neither the General Assembly nor the Security Council; it is the Secretariat Building, in which bureaucrats of many nations labor. Tours are conducted in several languages. The brick and glass Ford Foundation Building (above), designed by Kevin Roche, John Dinkeloo & Associates in 1967, includes an elaborate indoor garden. New York's West Side skyline (overleaf) shows just how prominent grand apartment buildings became in the city's life. Gentrification has come to the commercial streets—upper Broadway, Amsterdam Avenue, and Columbus Avenue—making the blocks of apartment buildings an even more desirable address.

Frederick Law Olmsted and Calvert Vaux turned wretched bogs, pig farms, and squatters' shacks into beautiful Central Park—New York's "backyard," forever protected from development. The bronze statue in the reflecting pool of the Conservatory Garden (opposite) is of Mary and Dickon from Frances Hodgson Burnett's The Secret Garden. *Originally cast in 1932, Paul Manship's bronze* Group of Bears *(top left) stands near the Friedman Playground. A favorite stop for brunch or dinner is the Tavern on the Green (bottom), which got a rare commercial spot in Central Park thanks to the pull of one of its first owners—Tammany Hall's "Boss" Tweed.* OVERLEAF: *The Bethesda Terrace is the only formal architectural element in Olmsted and Vaux's original plan. The centerpiece fountain features a bronze, winged* Angel of the Waters.

PREVIOUS PAGES:
A procession of
famous architects,
from Calvert Vaux to
John Russell Pope, had
a hand in the design
and expansions
of the American
Museum of Natural
History. It houses the
world's most extensive
collection of fossil
vertebrates, minerals,
gems, and meteor
fragments. Shipping
magnate Archibald
Gracie built his home
(top right) on the East
River in 1799. A
century later, the city
appropriated the
mansion for use as a
museum. During
Fiorello La Guardia's
administration it
became the mayoral
residence. BOTTOM:
Wallace Harrison
supervised several
architects on the
cluster of performing-
arts institutions
called Lincoln Center.
OPPOSITE: Sotheby's
auction house handles
all kinds of fine and
decorative arts, like
this seventeenth-
century Michael
Sweerts painting,
A Plague in an
Ancient City and
this French Royal
Silver tureen offered
at $7.5 million.

58

John Duncan's
memorial to Union
general Ulysses Grant
(above), popularly
known as "Grant's
Tomb," is modeled

after Napoleon's tomb
and other memorials.
Bronze busts in the
crypt, sculpted during
the Great Depression,
depict Grant's greatest

subordinates.
OPPOSITE: Daniel
Chester French's Alma
Mater, which was
completed in 1903
at the entrance to

Columbia University's
library, survived a
bomb blast during
violent student
demonstrations in
1968. The campus,

which is well con-
cealed behind fences
along upper Broadway
and Amsterdam
Avenue, is ringed by
coffeehouses and cafés.

LIBRARY·OF·COLUMBIA·UNIVERSITY

ALMA MATER

The Cotton Club nightclub (opposite) moved in 1978 from its original location to a spot under the entryway to the George Washington Bridge. The club still features blues and jazz on "Harlem's Main Street." Sylvan Terrace's 1882 row houses (left) are one of Upper Manhattan's finest addresses. They present "a revived memory of very old New York," according to the AIA Guide to New York City. Just across the street in a park stands the Morris-Jumel Mansion, built by Roger Morris as a summer residence. The mansion was George Washington's headquarters early in the Revolutionary War, but his forces were ousted from the home—and all of Manhattan— by the British. It became, among other things, a tavern before being pur- chased by a wealthy French merchant, Stephen Jumel.

Titles available in the Pictorial Souvenir series